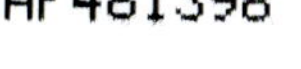
AF481398

The Christmas Children

Joanna Molloy

Dedication

Proceeds from The Christmas Children will benefit aid groups helping people, especially children, in the Middle East, Ukraine, and other locations now under duress:

The Red Cross [International Committee of the Red Cross] icrc.org

UNICEF [United Nations International Children's Emergency Fund]

unicef.org

The United Nations [U.N.] World Food Programme wfp.org

C.A.R.E. [Cooperative for Assistance and Relief Everywhere] care.org

Save the Children helps impoverished kids in the U.S. and globally. savethechildren.org

Americares provides healthcare in the U.S. and internationally americares.org

International Rescue Committee ICRC rescue.org

Barbershop Books, CNN Hero Alvin Irby, E.D., barbershopbooks.org

Acknowledgements

The Christmas Children
Story by Joanna Molloy
Illustrated by Amazon Kindle Publishing Artists and Joanna Molloy
Edited by Amazon Kindle Publishing Editors
Produced by Eamon Rush and
Produced by Eric Schneider, Amazon Kindle Publishing
With George Rush, Diane Molloy, Natasha Recoder, and Laura Recoder
Holland, Consultants

THE CHRISTMAS CHILDREN

Maria likes to play patty cake with her friend, Tasha. They chant:

⚜

"We're so lucky
We're so blessed
Yes, we have the very best.

We're so lucky
We're so blessed
Joy for all

That is our quest."

⚜

Now back home, Maria and her brother Zander write their letters to Santa Claus at the kitchen table as their mother bakes Christmas cookies.

"Mom, we've been good this year, haven't we?" Maria asks.

"Of course, you've been very good children this year," she responds. "What are you going to ask Santa for?"

"I really want a dolly with red hair!" Maria answers. "And a skateboard!"

"I want a football!" Zander announces. "And a new bike helmet!"

"Don't you want anything else?" their mother asks.

"I want lots of things!" Zander declares.

"So do I, but not for me," Maria says.

"What do you mean, Maria?" her mother asks.

Maria pauses for a moment before saying, "Well...I want to use the allowance I've saved up to buy a gift for a faraway child."

"A faraway child?" Mom asks. "Do you know this child?"

"No, I don't know them. But I know there are children out there who have had a rough year, and a gift might brighten up their day. I thought it would be great if we could share."

Her mother smiles with pride. "That's a great idea. There are many children out there who have had troubles this year. But, Maria, you cannot do this all by yourself."

Zander suddenly stands up and announces, "She's not alone. I'll help, too!"

Their mother smiles again and says, "You're good children. You should also ask your friends for help."

"OK, Mom," says Maria. She texts her friends to meet her at the toy shop."

Meanwhile, in the coldest reaches of the North Pole, the Elves are busy making games and toys for thousands of children.

Elf Jane ties a velvet ribbon in the curls of a doll named Calliope, whose shiny, long-lashy eyes open and close. She hums to herself:

Look how nicely I tied the ribbon in the curls.

This doll is such a great gift for one lucky girl.

Elves are silly and talk in rhymes, but they want to help Santa,
so they work till the clock chimes many times.
They climb knotted ropes and slide down fire poles
Finishing all the toys – that is their goal.

They make gadgets and gizmos, scooters and skates,
Pedal cars and puzzles just can't be late.
They make Legos and dolls and A-B-C blocks
Rocking horses, drums, and monkeys from socks.
They make guitars, action figures and they make games.
To make children happy; that is their aim

The Elves clack their hammers and they whirrr their saws.
They all focus closely and they rarely pause.
They paint pictures of princesses and ships with big sails
To put into golden books of fairy tales.

Baby Elf watches in wonder
At all of the prep
With snow globes and tinsel
He learns step-by-step
To make gingerbread houses
And cookies with icing
Candy canes and sugar plums
And Kiev cake for slicing.

Elf Maximillian says:
"But so many kids said Gimme Gimme
I doubt these will all fit down the chimneys!"

Supervisor DudleyDunn says:
"Hurry, hurry, hurry
I'm very worried
We won't complete the toys
For all the girls and boys."

Elf Gregor cries: "Now we have to oil the gears
Don't slow down to wiggle your ears.
There's no time to recite a rhyme!
Go, go, go, go. Here comes the snow show.
Go, go, go, go.   No time for cocoa!"

Always ready to lend a hand, Mrs. Claus is busy sewing an extra-cuddly teddy bear. She looks up at the clock and notices it's almost time for Santa to travel around the globe and deliver everyone their presents. So, she calls out to the Elves. "Elves, is your surprise ready for Santa yet?"

All the Elves shout together, "Yes, Mrs. Claus!"

Elf Andrewid takes the lead and says, "We're attaching it to Santa's sleigh right now!"

Meanwhile, back in her hometown, Maria and her dog, Sully, approach the toy shop, where they find her friends, Tasha and LuLu outside, looking through the glass at all the different toys.

LuLu points to a stuffed unicorn and says, "I love this one. I want it!"

Tasha marvels at a music box. She jumps, claps her hands, and adds, "I would love to get that!"

"But what should we get for the other kids?"

Maria responds, "That depends on how much money we have and what we can afford to get them. Let's go inside and take a better look."

As they enter the shop, Sully starts barking, "Woof! Woof! Woof!"

Maria tries to calm Sully down. "Shush, shush. Who's a good boy?"

But Sully has jumped up to put his paws on a shelf full of plush stuffed animals and is barking even louder now.

Maria says to her friends, "He thinks the plush stuffed kitty is real! Sully, shush now!"

"Hello, girls. How can I help you today?" asks Ms. Chillis, the storekeeper.

Maria steps forward and answers, "Well, I have my savings in my piggy bank and I would like to get a Christmas gift that costs this much." She shakes her piggy bank at an angle and coins land on the counter with a jingle and jangle.

Tasha and LuLu step up and say, "Don't worry. We brought our banks, too." Tasha shakes out her pink bunny bank, while LuLu empties her panda bank on the counter with a jangle and a jingle like the bells of Kris Kringle.

Ms. Chillis looks at the coins on the counters, impressed. "My goodness. You have saved up well! You should be proud of yourselves, girls. Let's count it up and see what you can buy, okay?"

Maria chants:

> "1-2-3-4
> Can we buy a little more?
> 5-6-7-8
> Maybe we can get some skates!"

Ms. Chillis asks, "Is this gift for yourselves?"

"No," the friends reply together.

Ms. Chillis looks at them, puzzled. "Who are you buying for?"

"We're here to buy gifts for children who have had rough or troubled times this year. We thought buying them gifts would cheer them up and bring them comfort and joy!" Maria explains.

"I see. And how do you plan to get these gifts to them?" Ms. Chillis asks with interest.

"We plan to put our gifts on Santa's sleigh," Tasha whispers. "Then, we hope that he'll take these gifts to children who need them but who might not be on his list."

Ms. Chillis smiles and says, "Well, that's a great plan, kids!"

The friends start to wander in the store, looking for treasure.

Maria walks through the aisles and grabs several toys, including a football, a soccer ball, puzzles, counting cards, board games, action figures, stuffed animals, doll clothes, a guitar, a baton, jacks, marbles, jump ropes, Legos, and more. She puts them on the counter and asks, "Can I get these?"

Donna, Ms. Chillis' fellow shopkeeper, is standing behind the counter now. She looks at all the toys Maria has picked and then at her coins and realizes she doesn't have enough money to buy them. She's about to say something when Ms. Chillis speaks up.

"You have exactly the right amount of money, down to the penny. Of course, you can get these!" Ms. Chillis says. She gives Donna a wink and Donna gives her a big smile. They are in the Spirit, too.

"Thank you, Ms. Chillis and Donna!" Maria, Tasha, and LuLu call out as they leave the Toy Shop with their arms full.

Maria returns home with her friends and they start wrapping the presents right away.

Zander then takes Sully and goes to meet his friends and he tells them the plan of kids giving to kids. They brainstorm and pitch ideas:

"How about we get them video games?"

"But how will we know what consoles they have?"

"You know what kids would like? Sneakers!"

"Sneakers are nice, but they'll cost too much,"

"Guys, I've got it. Why don't we set up a lemonade stand?"

"That's a great idea. We could sell other stuff there, too!"

"I could give up some of my video games,"

"I could sell my old controller,"

"I could sell some action figures!"

"I have two lightsabers. I can sell one!"

"Let's do it!"

Brian and Cale and Zander's other friends get a table and cloth and set up their stand in the center of town, while Henry brings the lemonade he's made.

The boys are busy with customers and Sully starts barking. "Woof! Woof!" He only wants one thing, and that's doggie biscuits Zander brought him. He jokes, "A tasket, a tisket, Sully wants a biscuit!"

The boys laugh together, and everyone pats Sully while he chomps.

In another town, Colleen, a teenage girl, is browsing social media on her phone when she sees a story about a group of boys and girls who want to give gifts to other children around the world.

Colleen sends a text to her friends. She invites them all to a Zoom meeting.

"Did you see what I shared with you?" Colleen asks curiously.

"Yes, I love that these kids are thinking of others even though they're far away," says Pam.

"Kids helping their fellow kids is so nice," says Jenn.

"Why don't we do something similar?" asks Colleen. "I was thinking we could bake cookies for Santa and buy gifts for the kids. We'll leave them together for Santa and hopefully when Santa takes a bite he'll read our note and bring the gifts to children who need them.

Ellen adds, "We can also knit hats, socks, sweaters, and gloves for the kids to help them stay warm." Everyone cheers her idea on.

"Sounds like a plan!" says Rachel.

Meanwhile, back up at the North Pole, Santa is feeling a little down. Mrs. Claus walks into their living room, only to find Santa sitting in his chair, gazing at the fireplace.

Mrs. Claus is worried about Santa. She asks him, "What's causing you woe, dear? You seem to have lost your get-up-and-go and your ho, ho, ho."

Santa doesn't look up. Sadness fills his voice. "I'm wondering if the spirit of Christmas is getting lost. Before, when children would send me letters, they used to ask me, 'How are you, Santa? How is Mrs. Claus? How are the Elves?' They would tell me about their families, which I always want to hear."

"And I remember when some children would ask for coats for their mothers, or toys for their brothers and sisters. This year they asked for so many presents, and just for themselves. Even the naughty ones did!!!" Santa paused for a moment. "I just hope that children haven't forgotten the true meaning of Christmas."

Mrs. Claus goes closer to Santa and pats him lovingly on the shoulder. "I hope they remember it's better to give than to receive. It will be all right."

Santa holds her hand on his shoulder and nods.

"It's almost Christmas Eve. Do you want some soup before you leave, or would you prefer cookies and cocoa before you go?" Mrs. Claus asks.

"Well, maybe I'll have a sip of cocoa to help my ho, ho, ho. Sometimes, the children leave me scrumptious cookies and if they do, I'll have those along the way."

"Well, my dear, you'll be happy to know that the Elves have a surprise for you." Mrs. Claus tells him. Santa's face lights up.

The Elves pop up in the room together and cry out, "Merry Christmas, Santa! Here's our gift for you!"

"Thank you, my good Elves, and Merry Christmas to you, too!" Santa says. "But what is this gift?"

Elf Duff steps forward and explains:

"It uses the power of solar
For all of us North Polers
It changes sun rays into fuel!
Like a log just in time for Yule!"

The other Elves all gather together, including Jack and Zach, Bloom and Klobes, Frank and Huck, Eric and Bertie, Chester and Andy, and they say, "Let's take an Elfie!" They pose for the picture.

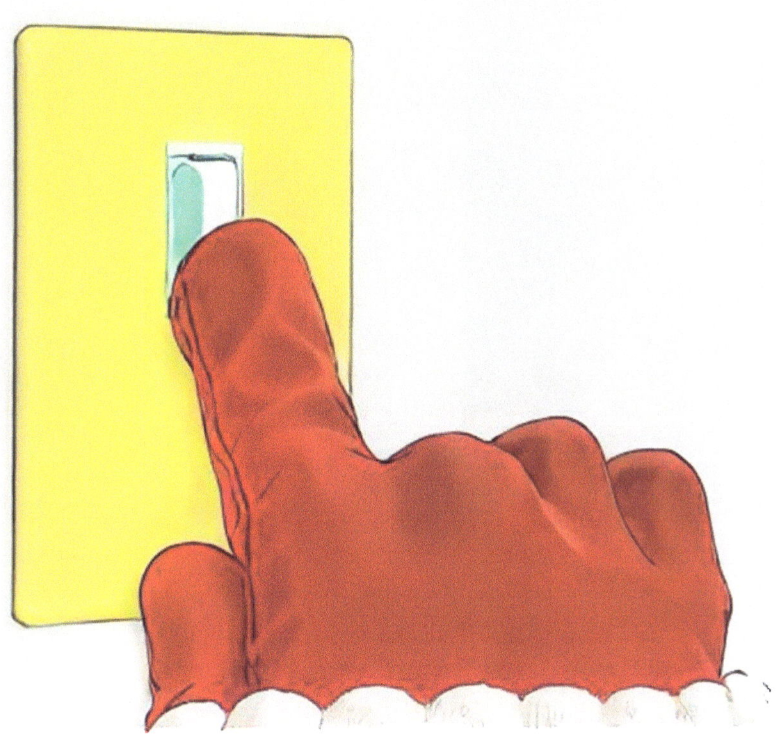

The camera flashes. Then, they shout together, "Press the switch, Santa. Turn it on!"

Joanna Molloy

The lights turn bright
The propellers twirl
To help Santa's sleigh fly
To every boy and girl

The engine goes Vroom!
The bells dong and ding
The drums boom boom
And the Elves begin to sing.

Santa is ecstatic
He says, "That is fantastic!
Thank you, Elves!
And now you know it's time to go.
It's starting to snow; ho, ho, ho!"

Baby Elf wants to go
But he must go to sleep
"You'll come next year," Santa says.
"That promise I will keep."

Santa gives Mrs. Claus a hug
Then he gives the reins a tug
The Elves hop up
And go on top

The Reindeer are psyched
To fly to their first stop.

Santa calls out: "Now, Dasher! Now, Dancer! Now, Prancer and Vixen! On, Comet! On Cupid! On, Donner and Blitzen! On, Ruby! On, Sierra! And Rudolph, too!

"Up and away, up and away!"

Down on land, Maria and her friends eagerly await Santa's arrival. They look up at the sky with binoculars through the snow. As soon as Maria spots Santa, she shouts, "Here comes Santa! He's nearly here. You can hear the reindeer bells! Hide! Jump in the snow forts! Don't let him spot you. Otherwise, he won't land here if he sees us. Remember, we're not allowed to see Santa!"

The kids all dash into the snow forts, but Sully doesn't follow them. Instead, he looks at the sky and continues barking, "Woof! Woof! Woof!"

"No, Sully!" says Maria. "You have to hide!   We're in the snow fort, come inside!

"Don't be silly, Sully! Don't be a naughty doggie!" Maria whispers.

"He wants to play with the Reindeer!" whispers Zander.

Santa lands in front of a house
and brings his bag down the chimney
He smiles at the sight
The Christmas tree
It is lit up bright

A choo-choo train chugs
Around the lights
There are sweets and treats
To give holiday bliss
In the doorway hangs mistletoe
To encourage a kiss.

Santa then fills the stockings with care.
He places the presents under the tree
and hopes the children there will share.

While Santa is inside
The children no longer hide
They run with their gifts
To put on the sleigh on this special day.

Sully runs up, and a Reindeer nuzzles him.

"Hey, hey, hey!" Elf Joey yells.
"Get away from the sleigh!
Putting things on it is not OK!
Explain yourselves, I daresay!"

Caught red-handed in the act, Maria and Zander exchange nervous glances. Then, Maria looks at Elf Joey and explains, "Sorry, Mr. Elf. We were hoping to place some gifts on Santa's sleigh so that Santa – and you – could deliver them to children around the world who need good things this year more than ever."

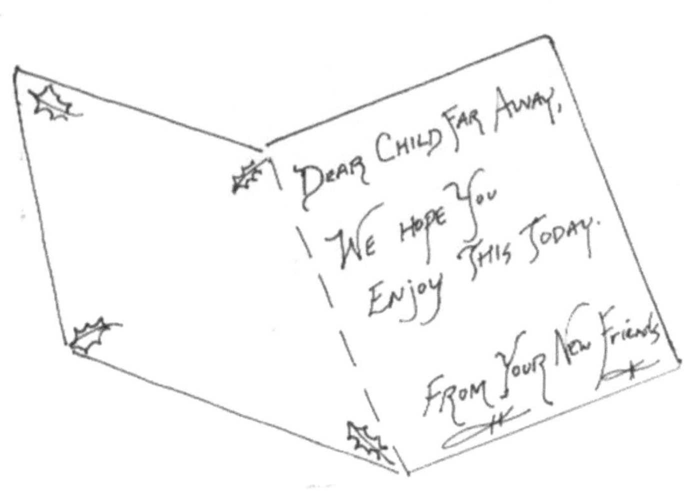

Maria shows him the note they put on Santa's sleigh. It reads:

"Dear Child Far Away,
We hope you enjoy this gift today.
From Your New Friends."

Elf Joey knows this doesn't happen often
and soon, his mood begins to soften.

"All right," Elf Joey says, "but run home now and go to sleep, or we won't be able to deliver your presents. You know that children cannot be awake when Santa comes to their house!"

The children all run home, and only then does Santa come outside. He looks at his sleigh, notes the extra presents, and asks,

"What are all these extra presents, Elfie?"

Elf Joey answers, "Children put these gifts on the sleigh
And ask that you deliver them to kids far away.
Kids who this year have had it rough
Now they'll get some special stuff.

Over the cities and over the prairies
Santa, this will make you merry.
Hey, hey, yay, yay!
We'll have to make more stops.
Before the light of day."

Santa looks at Elf Joey with delight. "This is the best present I could have asked for. I was afraid that the children had forgotten about the true meaning of Christmas, but I guess I was wrong. These are children who have the real Christmas spirit. Prepare yourself, my good Elf! We have gifts to deliver! Ho, ho, ho! Come on, Reindeer, through the snow! Off around the world, we go."

≹ 38 ≹

Santa's loud, booming voice fills the air before they fly out of sight. He exclaims:

"Peace on Earth to All!
And to All, a Good Night!"

Epilogue

Santa says to the Elves on the sleigh:

"From high up here
We see our Beautiful Earth
Our blue and green marble
Spinning slow
Elf Eamon, with the poet's eyes
Please tell us what you see below."

Joanna Molloy

"Well, Santa,
Before the Dawn pulls back
Its pale sheer curtain
There is one thing we will see for certain
And that's the wonderful world we share
From oceans to mountains
Through fields and forests
And even throughout the air.

From high up with the shooting stars
Hear music from the heart of Space
The singing bowls and gongs and chimes
That help us meditate.

The Christmas Children

They will heal and give you calm
And make you feel sublime
You can hear the angels chant
To give you some peacetime.
La la la ohm
Dong dong dong dong
Ding ding ding ding
Sing sing sing song.

And from our Flyer
We hear Choirs
Sing harmony down below.

The families sing carols with
Snow Men and Snow Women
And Snow Kids who sing all aglow!

Joanna Molloy

We'll see magic and miracles
Of Nature and humankind
Adventures and inventions
That make us feel lyrical
Spectacles that will blow your mind

See the Narwhals wave goodbye to us
With their special spiral tusks
Now, polar bears across the tundra
Soon, koala bears Down Under.

There's aurora borealis
Like a colored sky palace
And above is Polaris
The North Star to guide us.

The sacred sky is sprinkly
With stars that are twinkly
Like Orion whose sword
You can see quite distinctly.

There's Cassiopeia who gives the idea
She's a queen with the shape of a crown
But she was conceited
So she got defeated by
Nymphs on sea horses they rode up and down.

And the mountains magnificent
Are really significant:
The Alps; Himalayas; the Andes;
Karakorams in Kashmira;
Fuji; Rockies; and Sierras,
And a mountain made of rock candy.

And tumbling down them all
Rush blue waterfalls
A foamy arcade in fantastic cascade
Into rivers and lakes
And stacked rice-paddy cakes.

The Christmas Children

There're the Black Hills
where dinosaurs roamed and flew
Triceratops and Pterodactyls
And a giant T-Rex named Sue.

There are forests so lush
You can hear a peaceful thrush
And the nightingales sing
As our Reindeer bells ring

And in their deserts vast
They sandboard and dune bash
The Kalahari and the Gobi
Sahara, Arabian, and Mojave.

See oases with water where they can grow plums
On a thorny cactus sits a desert sand cat
Over there are some camels who have double humps
They're called dromedaries – what's better than that?

We see meadows with flowers
That bloom in the cold
Periwinkle and primrose
Pop up so bold.

Witness Redwood trees as wide as a car
Baobob trees in Madagascar
There are coconuts atop palms in the tropics
Seeing monkeys grab them is a top TV topic.

There are bonsai trees manicured to be teeny
And Christmas trees that smell ever-greeny
I hope folks plant more trees in the new year
To bring beloved Earth even more cheer.

See elephants and rhinos
In Africa amazing
Giraffes and hippos
And striped zebras grazing.

Joanna Molloy

Spot lions and tigers
And other big cats
Leopards and panthers
And cheetahs run fast.

And deep in the sea
Are the giant blue whales
Listen close, and you'll hear
They're singing their scales.

Here are clouds like marshmallows
Full of snow soon to flurry
But on Christmas Eve, we like that
That's never a worry.

The geese are migrating
In the shape of a Vee
Flocks of parrots and quetzals
In red, blue, and green.

The eagles fly with wingspans so wide
Same with the owls
At night, when they glide.

There's a muster of marabous
A colony of caribous
And bluebirds that fly
Over the rainbows.

There are Great Blue Heron and swan
Who watches over their eggs
While pink flamingos
Can stand on one leg!

There are walruses, turtles;
Manatees, seals,
The Lion's Mane Jellyfish
Just doesn't seem real!

The Christmas Children

When we reach the South Pole
We'll see penguins so neat
They keep babies warm
Sitting them on their feet

Pink dolphins in the Amazon
In the Caribbean, tropical fish,
Fireflies and ladybugs
If one lands, make a wish.

There fly bumblebees and honeybees
Yes, there is a difference.
And Monarchs are the butterflies
Who fly so great a distance.

The shepherds watch over their
Cows, goats, and sheep
From morning till night
When their babies fall asleep.

Some furry animals run free in the woods
Seeing fox, squirrels and chipmunks
Makes you feel good.

See hedgehogs and porcupines
Racoons and baboons
Lemurs and beavers
Those clever dam weavers.

Farmers grow apples
Oats, soybeans and corn
They grow wheat to make bread
And work hard every morn.

They get eggs from their chickens
Who go cluck cluck cluck
And the rooster who crows
Is said to bring luck.

Joanna Molloy

See what's been created by people:
Minarets, domes, temples,
And stained-glass cathedrals.

They have built skyscrapers
Both needle and Deco
Stunning bridges and tunnels
When you hoot, there's an echo.

There is the Sphinx
And Alhambra mosaics
The Acropolis, the Taj Mahal
That's nothing prosaic!

The art that they've made will
Make you say 'pinch me'
Picasso, Michelangelo and
Leonardo da Vinci.
Da Vinci made Mona Lisa
But also, inventions
And today scientists take us
To another dimension.

They're healing the sick
And saving our lives
They even make rockets
To blast through the skies.

And look at those athletes
Who play baseball and hockey
Teams play cricket and football
They race horses with jockeys.

They can skateboard and surf
Play soccer on turf
They play tennis and hoops
And swim relays in groups.

Even young bambinos

Ride palominos
They do cartwheels and flips
And double ropes skip.

Hear the music people make
With pianos and harps
Horns, strings, and kora
Notes minor or sharp.

Just one busker can sound so celestial
Music might be the thing
That makes people most special.

They dance salsa, flamenco
Tap, breakdance, and tango,
And twirling in the Nutcracker ballet
Ballerinas in tutus on Christmas Day.

And actors pretend
On the screen or the stage
Keeping Shakespeare alive
For many an age.

How do they get us to laugh and to cry?
It's magic, I tell you
'Cause I don't know why.

Oh, say, can you see
people created democracy
Instead of aristocracy
So everyone could be free.

"What a wonderful world!" Santa says.

The End. Or is it the Beginning?

About The Author

Joanna Molloy was a staff journalist at New York magazine, the New York Post, and the New York Daily News, and she has written several books for grownups. A nonfiction book she co-authored, The Greatest Beer Run Ever, was on the New York Times bestseller list for six months, and was made into a 2022 Skydance Apple Originals movie of the same title starring Zac Efron, Bill Murray, and Russell Crowe, directed by Peter Farrelly, and produced by Andrew Muscato. She wrote and illustrated this book, The Christmas Children, to help raise money for aid groups in the Middle East, Ukraine, and other troubled places in our world, and is grateful to those who purchase it. Proceeds will benefit the Red Cross, icrc.org; UNICEF, unicef.org; the United Nations World Food Programme, wfp.org; Save the Children, savethechildren.org; C.A.R.E. [Cooperative for Assistance and Relief Everywhere], care.org; International Rescue Committee, rescue.org; Americares, americares.org; Barbershop Books, CNN Hero Alvin Irby, barbershopbooks.org. The author is also grateful to Eric Schneider and his team at Amazon Kindle Self-Publishing for their amazing talent and dedication. She is also proud that this book is printed by Amazon in America.

The author is grateful to Executive Director Eric Schneider and Art Director Sean Williams and their teams at Amazon Kindle Self-Publishing